Introduction

The SPIN: 360° project began in 2015, and was conceived as an on-going conversation. To date it has comprised the following: a published monograph; numerous national and international lectures; events; exhibitions; a growing Instagram feed; a specially brewed beer; extensive Spotify playlists; and now this—an occasional publication that looks at aspects of Spin's studio work that might otherwise go unrecorded or unexplored.

The journal format offers the studio a vehicle to share aspects of our culture, and allows us to form a record of our creative interests and outputs—the stuff that normally goes unseen.

Beginnings

When a studio moves to a new space, as we recently have, it offers the possibility of a new beginning. Environment, good or bad, influences us all. We recently moved from a very nice but conventional studio space to a slightly more idiosyncratic set up. Our new space is purpose built, surrounded by plants of varying types, literally a breath of fresh air, inspiring us to develop our work. A new optimism abounds, like a garden in full bloom.

As a result, the idea of new beginnings is very much front and centre of our minds, and underpins the second issue of SPIN: Adventures in Typography.

Both serious and silly in equal measure (occasionally at the same time), this project sees us searching for the new and the surprising, fresh air and joy, within typography. We have spent time making by computer and by hand—analogue and digital in concert—to capture the feeling of the unexplored possibilities that lie ahead.

This mix of experimentation and play allows us to make work that is outside our comfort zone. Failure doesn't seem so scary as we give each other the support and confidence to push ourselves collectively. We found the process exhilarating and challenging and we hope you that you find it inspiring.

COUNTING OFF

THE BEATLES:
I SAW HER STANDING
THERE.
1−2−3−4

THE BEATLES:
TAXMAN.
1 2 3 4−1 2

THE BEATLES:
A DAY IN THE LIFE
(ANTHOLOGY 2).
SUGAR PLUM FAIRY,
SUGAR PLUM FAIRY.

THE BEATLES:
SGT. PEPPER'S
LONELY HEARTS CLUB
BAND (REPRISE).
1 2 3 4

BECK:
ELEVATOR MUSIC.
1 2 YOU KNOW
WHAT TO DO.

DAVID BOWIE:
BOYS KEEP
SWINGING.
1 2 3 4

GET UP (I FEEL
LIKE BEING A) SEX
MACHINE.
CAN I COUNT IT
1 – 2 – 3 – 4 !

CHIC:
LE FREAK.
1 – 2 AAA
FREAK

THE CLASH:
CLAMPDOWN.
1 2 3 4

THE CLASH:
JAIL GUITAR DOOR
1 2 3 4

THE CLAS
(WHITE M
HAMMERS
PALAIS.
1 2 1 – 2

ELVIS C
SEVEN
WEEKEND.
1 – 2 – 3 – 4 – 5 – 6 – 7

CREAM:
MOTHER'S LAMENT.
A 1 – A A 2 – A A 3 – A
4

J SHADOW:
THE NUMBER SONG.
3 4 5 – BREAK
D BY.

EL HT
OR R
A E WORLD.
1 2

TH MING LIPS:
U REALIZE??
3 4

FLIPPER:
NOTHING.
OK. 1...WAIT, EVERYONE
START AT THE SAME
TIME READY?
1 2

WHEEL
1 2 3 4

JOY DIVIS...
WARSAW.
3 – 5 – 0 – 1 ...

KRAFTWERK:
NUMBERS.
EINS, ZWEI, DREI,
VIER, FÜNF, SECHS,
SIEBEN, ACHT.

JJ CALE:
CRAZY MAMA.
1 2 3 4

KESHA:
BASTARDS
1 2 3 4

JOHN LENNON:
I DON'T WANNA
FACE IT.
UN, DEUX, EINS—
ZWEI—HICKLE—
PICKLE.

JOHN LENNON
AND THE PLASTI...
ONO BAND:
GIVE PEACE
A CHANCE.
2 – 1 2 3 4

THE MODERN LOVERS:
ROADRUNNER.
1 2 3 4 5 6

CHRIS MONTEZ:
LET'S DANCE.
1 2 – 1 2 3

NEW RADICALS:
YOU GET WHAT
YOU ...
... 1 2 3 OW.

...RASPBERRY BERET.
1 2 1 ... 3 – 4

PIXIES:
I'VE BEEN TIRED.
1 ...

ELVIS PRESLEY:
BLUE SUEDE SHOES.
WELL, IT'S A ONE FOR
THE MONEY, TWO FOR
THE SHOW, THREE TO
GET READY, NOW GO,
CAT, GO.

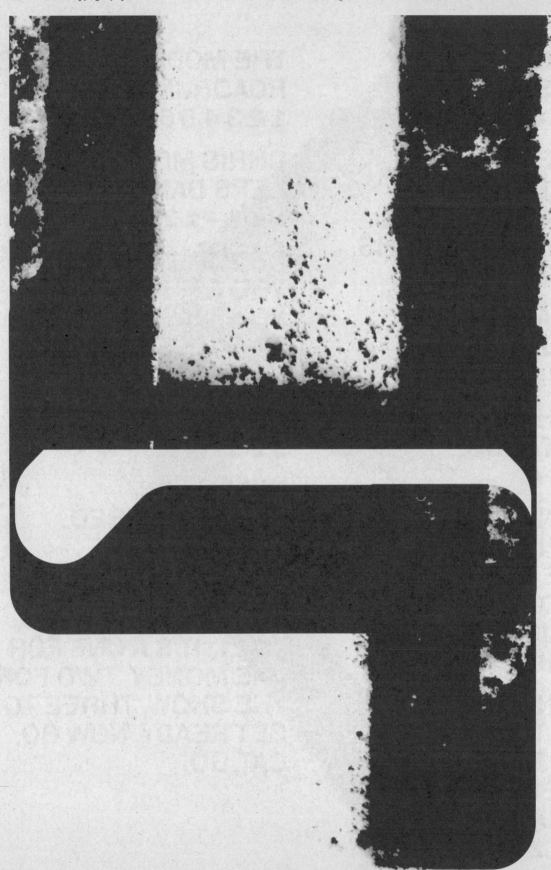

THE RAMONES:
SHEENA IS A
PUNK ROCKER.
GO.

SAM THE SHAM &
THE PHARAOHS:
WOOLY BULLY.
UNO, DOS. ONE,
TWO, TRES, CUATRO.

THE TEMPTATIONS:
BALL OF CONFUSION.
1 2 – 1 2 3 4

THEY MIGHT BE
GIANTS:
(SHE WAS A) HOTEL
DETECTIVE.
1 2 3 4

THE THE:
I'VE BEEN WAITIN'
FOR TOMORROW
(ALL OF MY LIFE).
10 9 8 6 5 4 3 2 1 0

U2:
VERTIGO.
UNOS, DOS, TRES,
CATORCE.

WIRE:
12XU.
12XU.

WILSON PICKETT:
LAND OF 1000
DANCES.
1 2 3 – 1 2 3

THE WHITE STRIPES
AS UGLY AS I SEEM
2 3

BRUCE SPRINGSTEEN:
FROM SMALL THINGS
(BIG THINGS ONE
DAY COME)
A 1 2 3 4 – 1 2 3 4

X–RAY SPEX:
OH BONDAGE!
UP YOURS!
SOME PEOPLE THINK
LITTLE GIRLS
SHOULD BE SEEN
AND NOT HEARD
BUT I SAY...
OH BONDAGE!
UP YOURS!
1 2 3 4

So here we are the very beginning. We have dug deeper into the formal properties of type in this issue, exploring the possibilities of each idea, employing, in some ways a more traditional and rigorous methodology. The original thought for A:F/F (Alien: Future/Font) was to make an organic, fluid face that is built upon deliberately perverse foundations. The proportions are inconsistent and odd, the forms are elastic. We asked ourselves whether it could continually morph without losing its essential characteristics. Legibility wasn't a concern as much as a curiosity. In fact it wasn't clear if it would be legible in any shape of form until it was quite a way down the road. We imagined it as a futuristic programmable font with thousands of characters that would constantly redesign itself.

LET'S START AT THE VERY BEGINNING

WHEN YOU READ YOU BEGIN WITH

A VERY GOOD PLACE TO START

Do Re Mi
Sound of music
Richard Rogers and Oscar Hammerstein II
(This spread works best if you sing along)

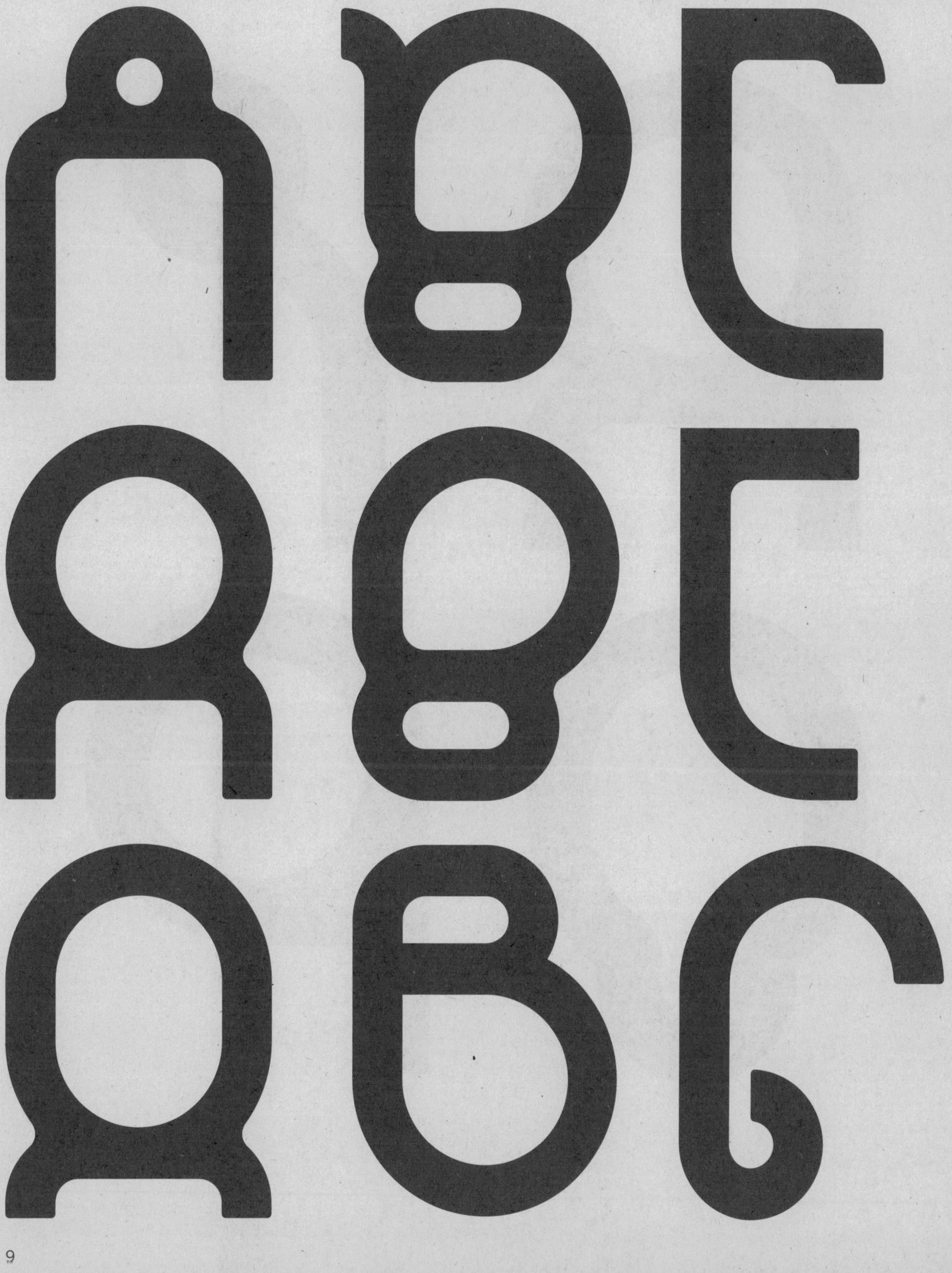

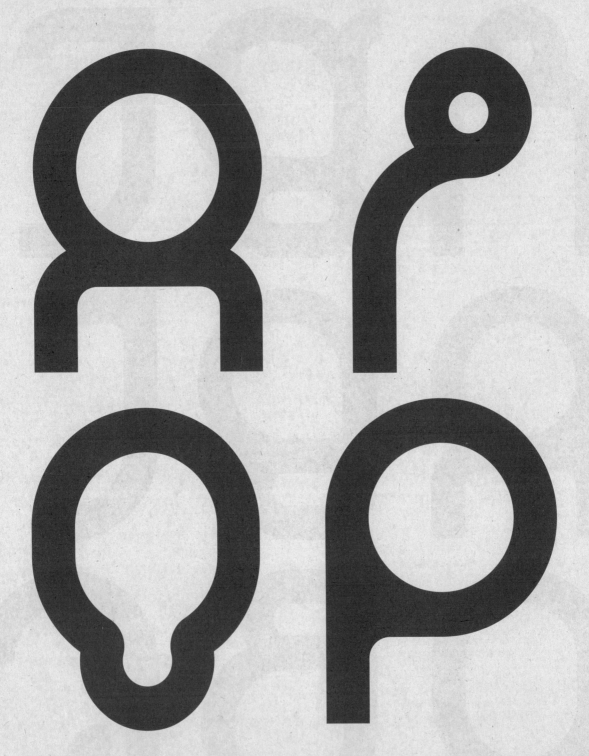

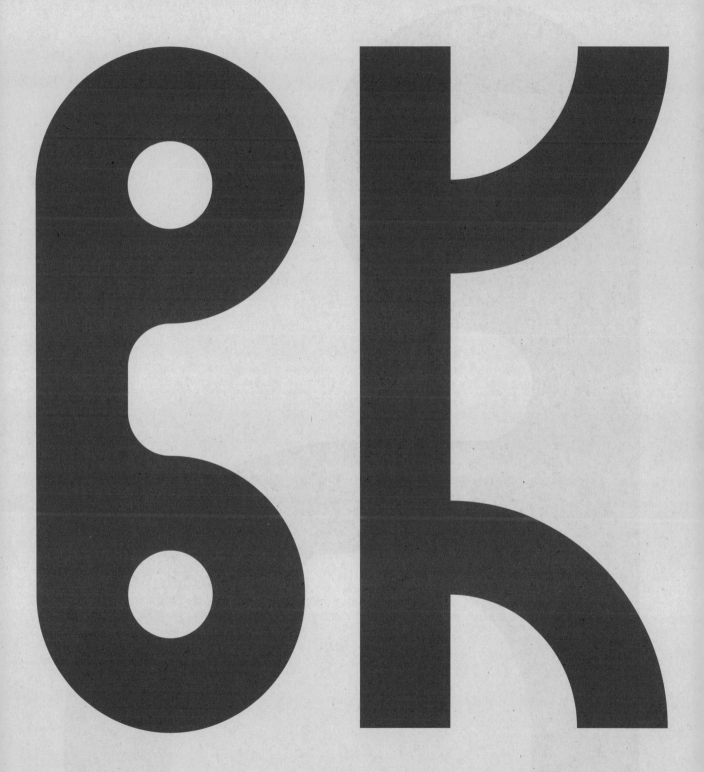

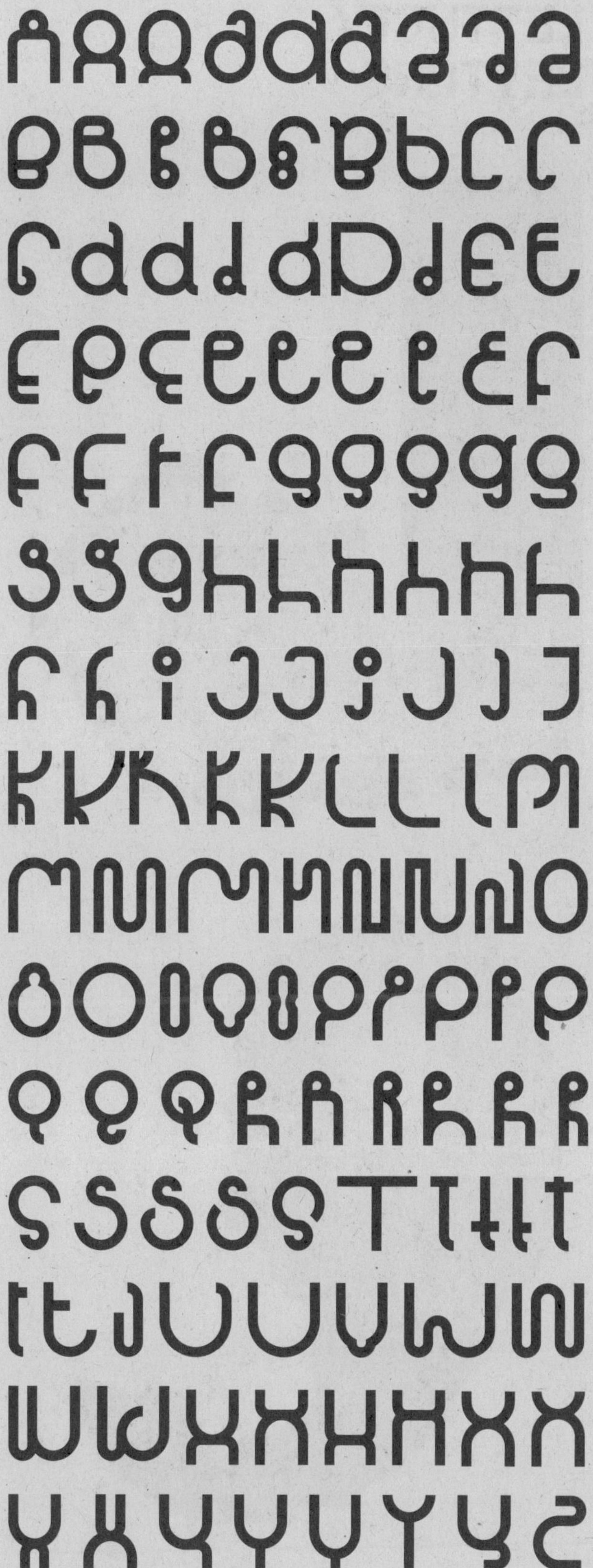

LETTUCE/
LETTERS

Earlier this year we realised a long standing desire to create a studio environment that allows us to bring work and life closer together. To this end, we moved the studio into a purpose-built space at the bottom of our garden. A big part of this ambition was to have a garden and grow vegetable and herbs in it. It is early days but we have had moderate success with courgettes, chillies, chives, lettuce, mint, oregano, rosemary and sage. Next year we hope to expand our repertoire of ingredients and build a bigger menu around our produce. The following lettering was, unsurprisingly inspired by our new surroundings.

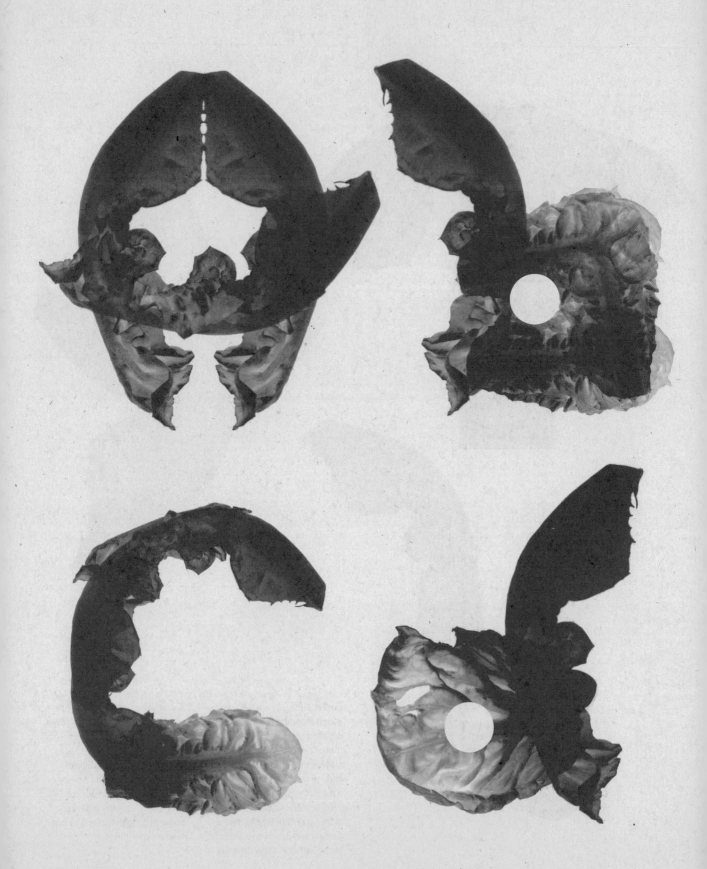

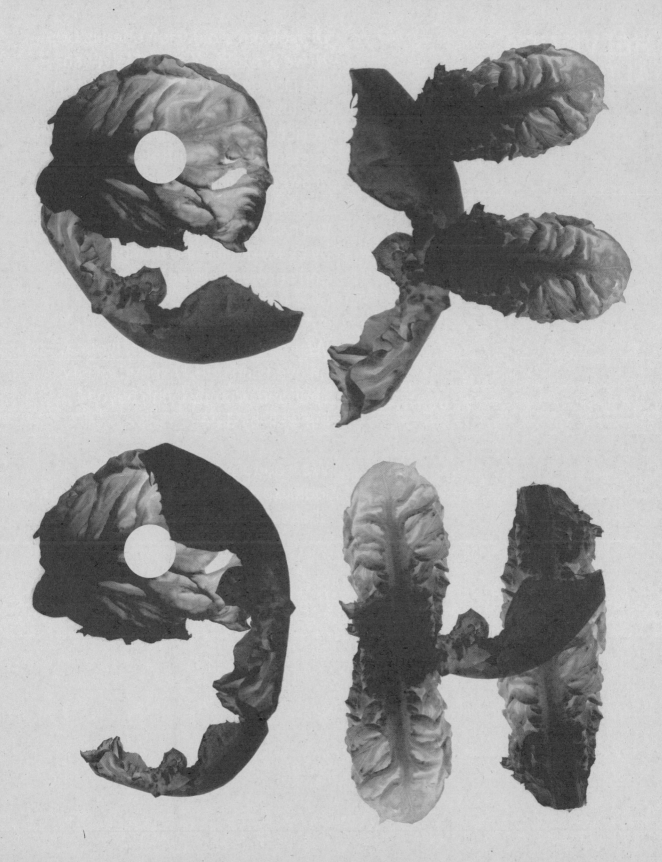

HELVETICA ALT

Or Helvetica old. Helvetica is 60, so we are told. What if, Helvetica like Dorian Gray, has been passing her time away in a dusty attic in Zurich. Gently fading away in an ancient wooden Letterpress drawer, steadily ageing over the years, becoming shrivelled and worn-out. Increasingly exhausted by every designer's thoughtless and careless abuse and incessant over use.

We imagined poor old Helvetica, unloved and utterly spent, crusty, sour and grumpy living beyond her sell-by date.

We wondered, what would she look like after such a life? Wrecked, shaky, a little crumpled?

23

25

27

33

35

37

45

47

53

55

57

65

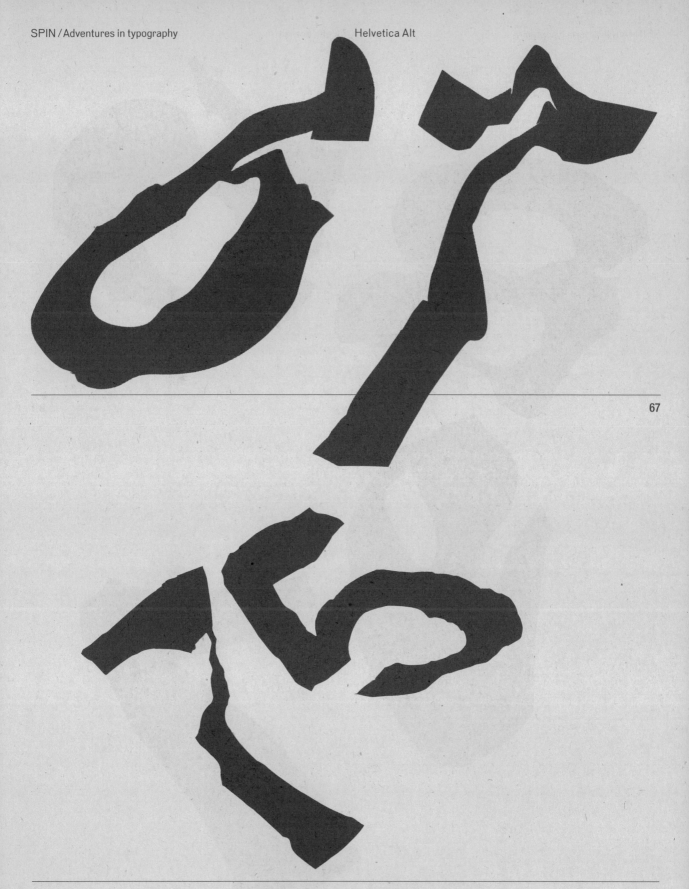

85

97

DR FRANKENSTEIN'S HELVETICA

The Helvetica reverie continues. Was there, we wondered, a drop of creative juice left to be squeezed out of the limp and battered body? A dead cat bounce, one final hurrah?

As the pulse grows weaker, could some urgent, drastic intervention, performed by skilled graphic surgeons help a dire situation? By the taking of a glimmering razor-sharp 10a scalpel blade and some injudicious, delicious, malicious manhandling, could the old girl be rescued? Was there a slim hope that the slicing and dicing of the grande old dame may bring her crapulous corpse, hideously distorted, back to life? I'm sure that similar thoughts were entertained by Dr Frankenstein for his, by happy coincidence, Swiss monster.

Well, we gave it a go.

Boris Karloff who played Frankenstein's monster in the 1931 film 'Frankenstein' (pictured opposite) was born in Camberwell, a suburb of South London, and originally rejoiced in the moniker of William Henry Pratt. He was very proud of his English heritage and by all accounts a bit of a Cricket buff, often watching the game at the Oval Cricket ground, also in South London.

The following text comes from the trailer for the film.

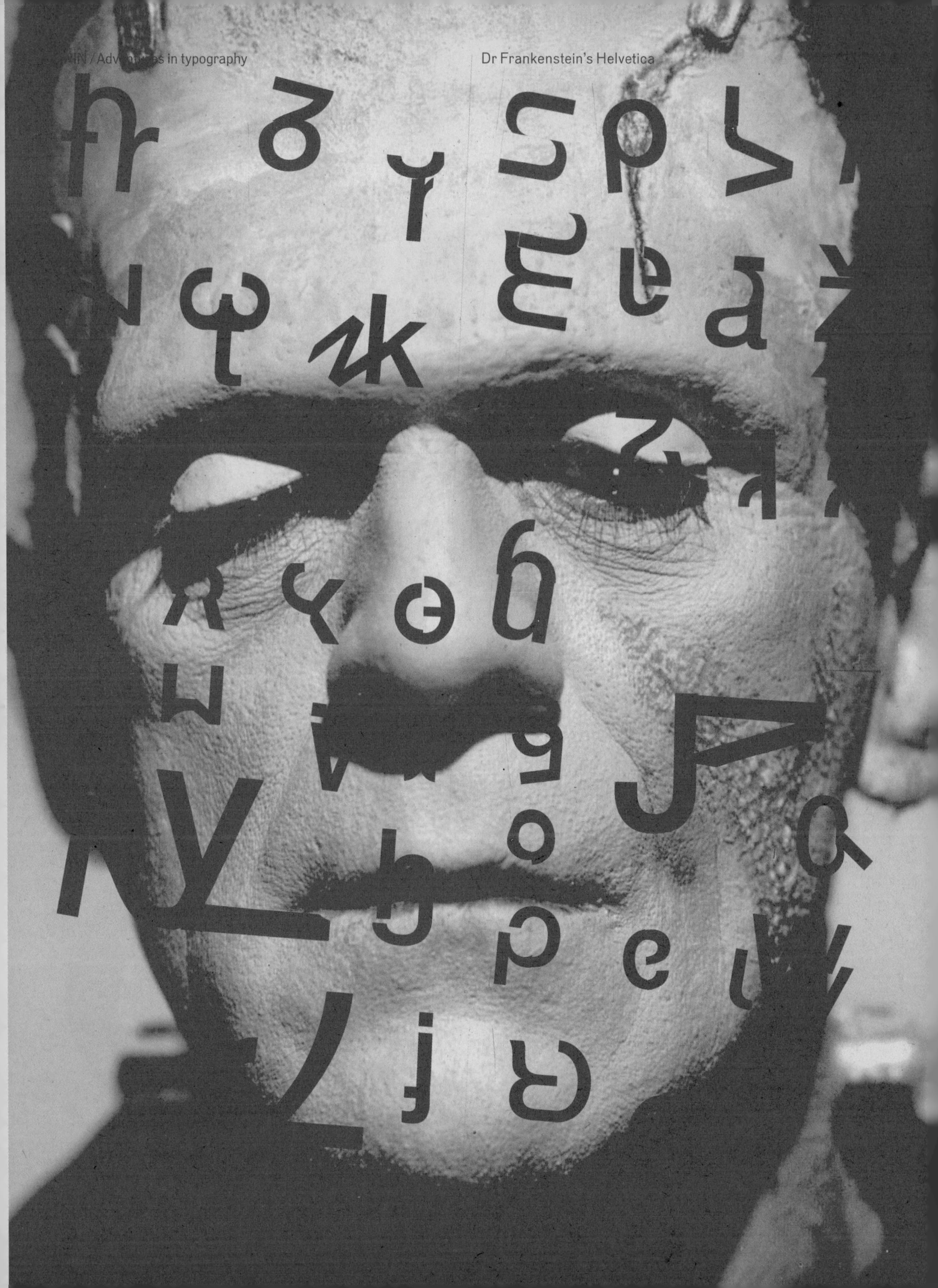

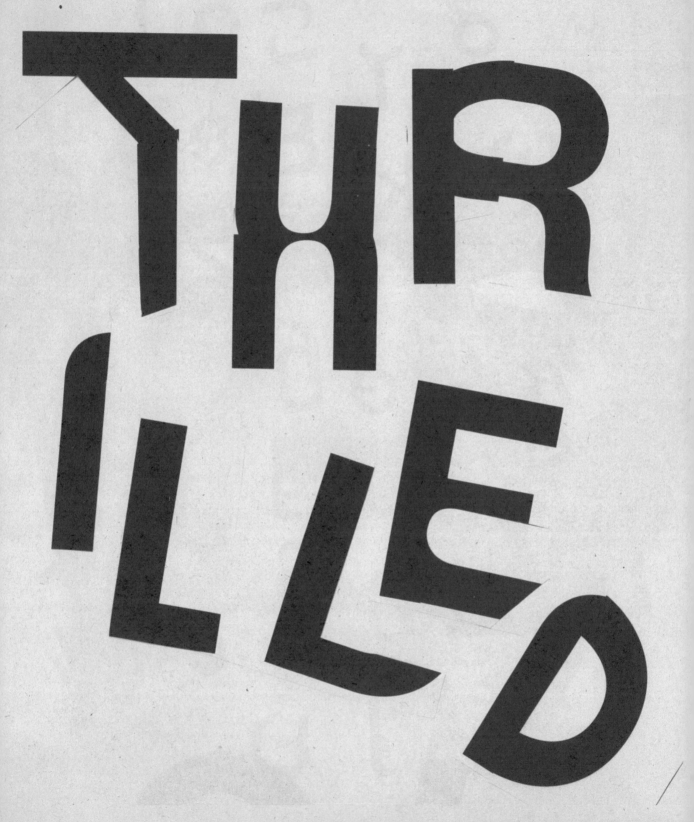

THRILLED

Millions have been thrilled
Millions are waiting to be thrilled...

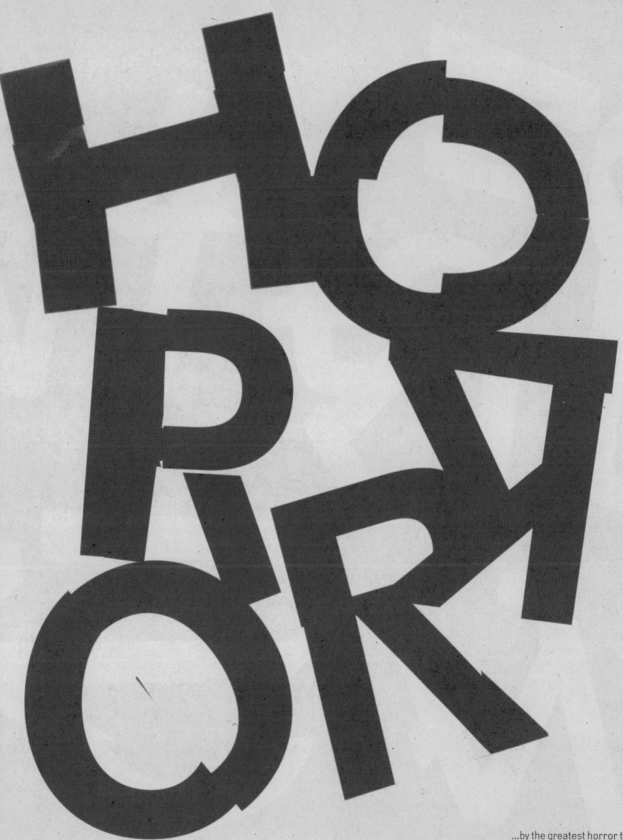

...by the greatest <u>horror</u> the
screen has ever known!

...Frankenstein

Terrifying fiendish Never monster

See Karloff in his most
terrifying performance...
...as the fiendish monster...
...and you'll know why there
can never be another...
Frankenstein

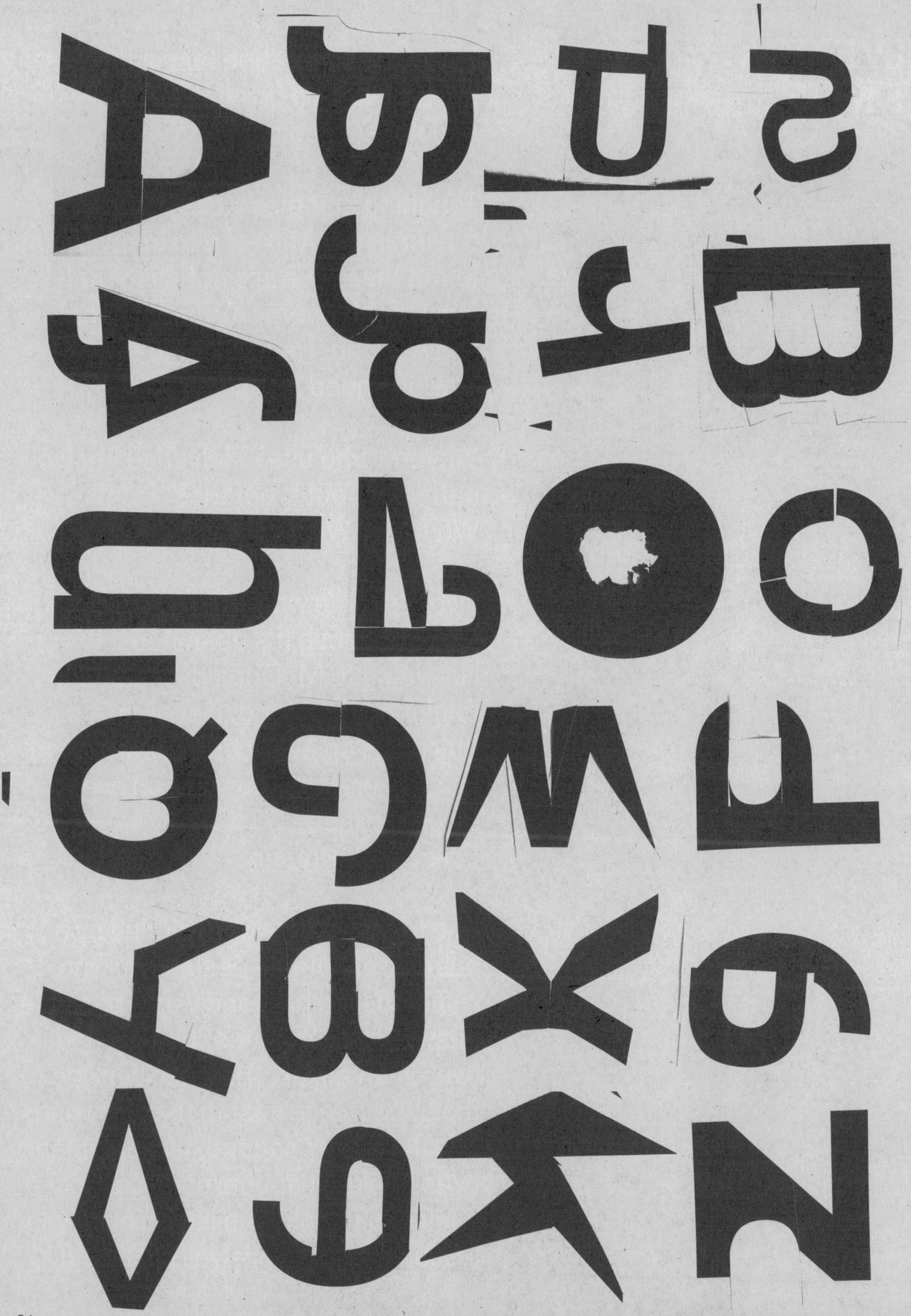

HELVETICA
EST MORT

Sadly, the operation failed, it turns out that we are graphic designers and not surgeons.

Touching eulogies were found on the internet. And as with many things found there, we are not absolutely sure of their veracity, but let's not allow the desire for truth get in the way of a good story:

'Anyone who uses Helvetica knows nothing about typefaces'.
Wolfgang Weingart

'Most people who use Helvetica, use it because it's ubiquitous. It's like going to McDonalds instead of thinking about food. Because it's there, it's on every street corner, so let's eat crap because it's on every street corner'.
Erik Spiekermann

The funeral was well attended by a number of notable designers, who remembered her fondly as a possible answer to every question they had ever been asked. After the service the ashes were cast to the four winds, and, for a split second, through bleary eyes, the dust appeared to collect itself into the old familiar form. It was just an illusion. Farewell old friend.

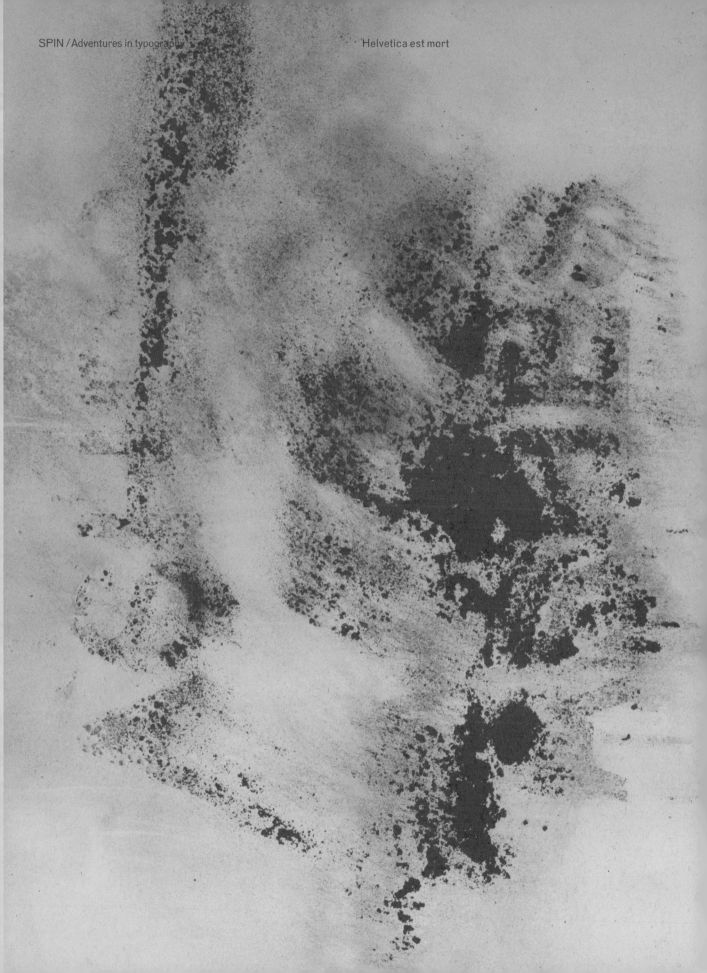

TAPE
FACE

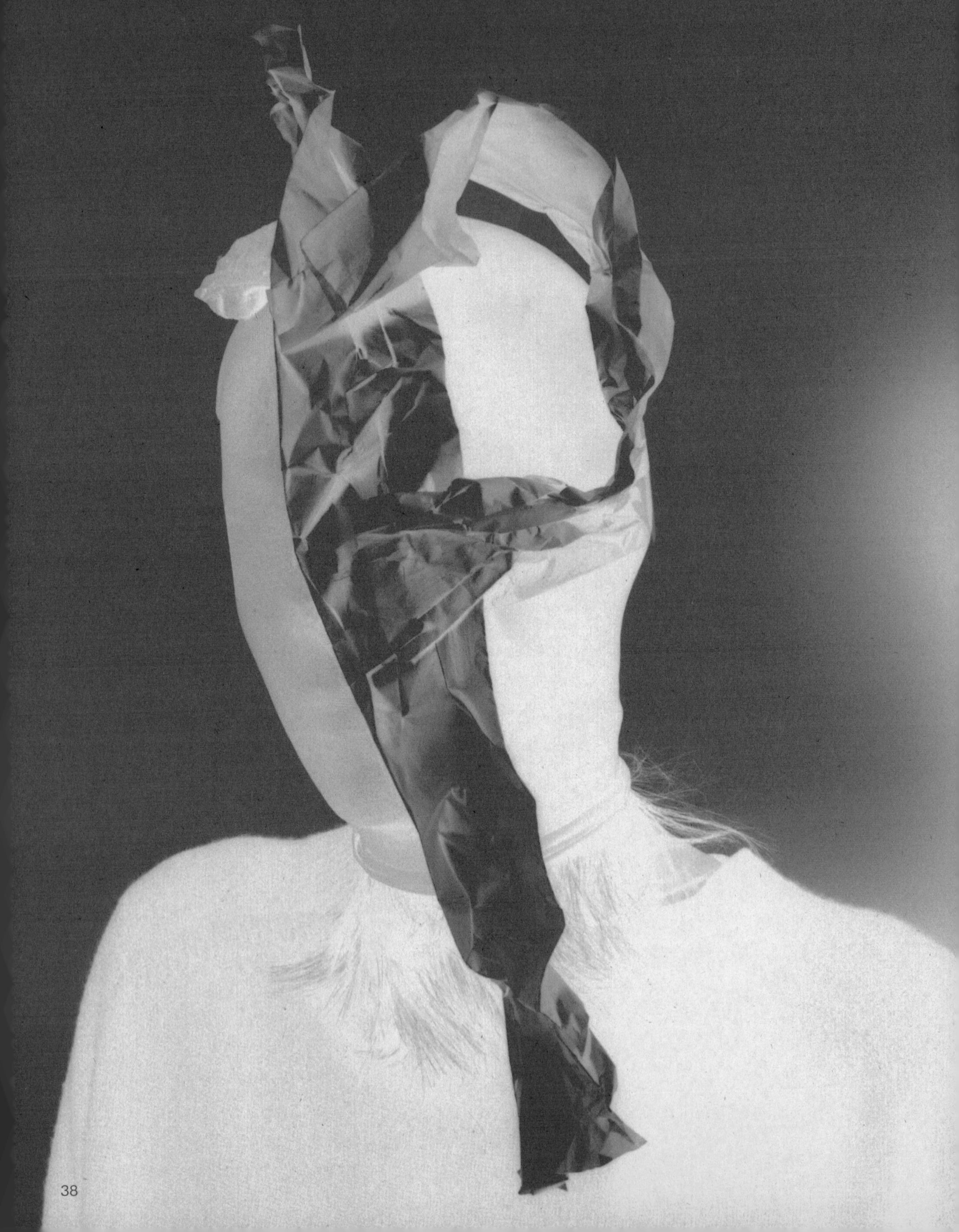

STRIPEY
FACE

Stripey Face Bold.
With apologies to
Franco Grignani

Stripey Face Bold Freestyle

BODY
TEXT

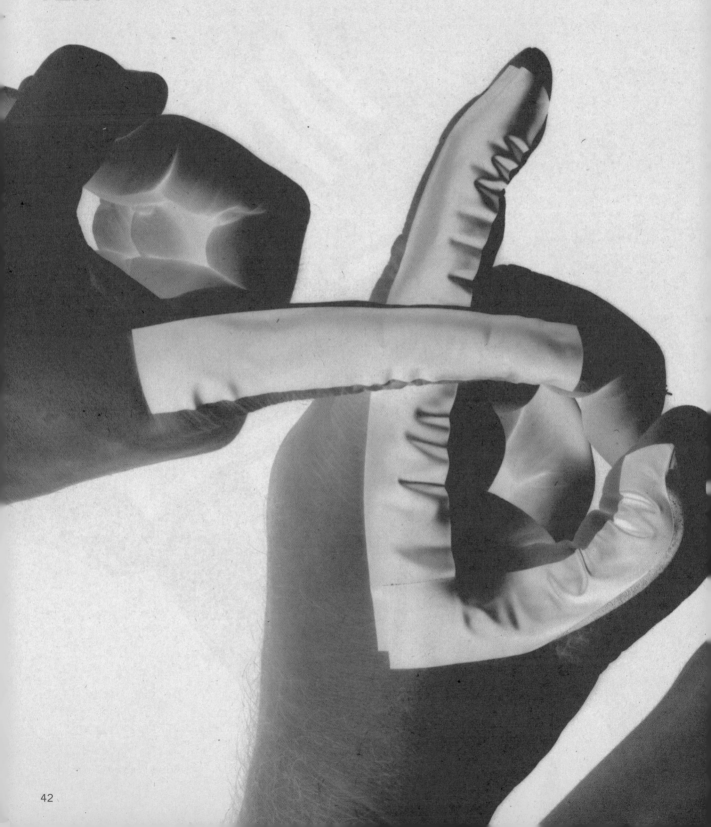

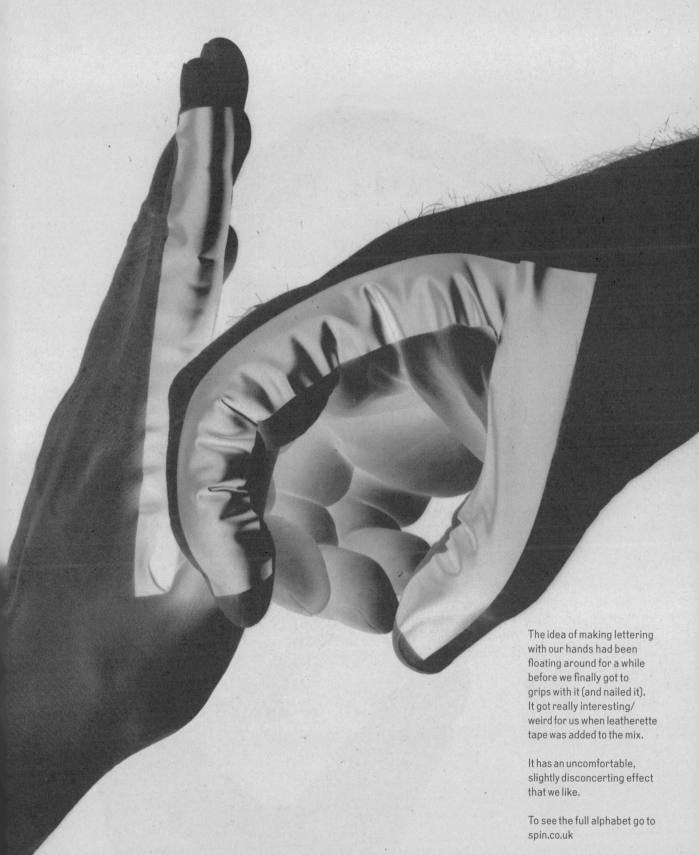

The idea of making lettering
with our hands had been
floating around for a while
before we finally got to
grips with it (and nailed it).
It got really interesting/
weird for us when leatherette
tape was added to the mix.

It has an uncomfortable,
slightly disconcerting effect
that we like.

To see the full alphabet go to
spin.co.uk

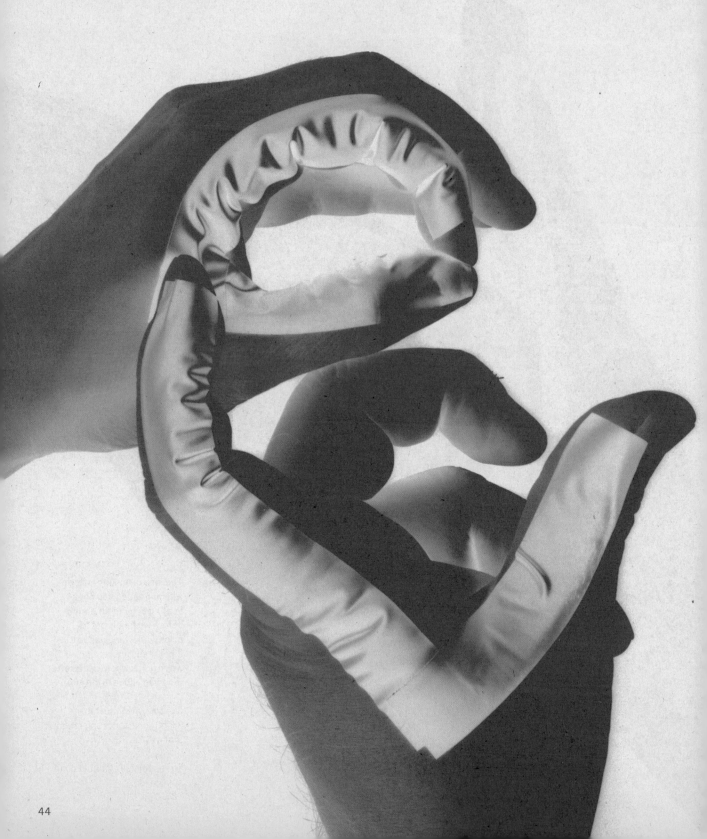

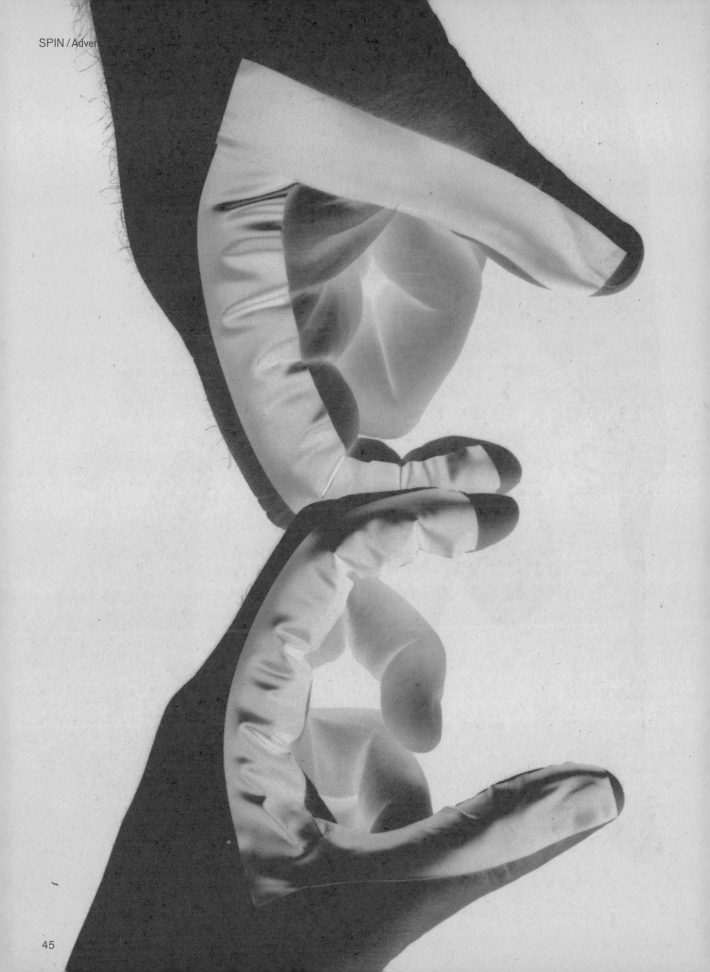

SPIN /
Adventures in typography
Issue 002

Colophon

Magazine design/concept:
Tony Brook, Claudia Klat,
Jonathan Nielsen

Words:
Tony Brook

Editor:
Adrian Shaughnessy

Production manager:
Edie Lippa

Publishing director:
Patricia Finegan

Printer:
Generation Press

Typeface:
Dada Grotesk by Optimo

Paper stocks:
Newsprint
Amvera FTP
Glassine

For information on
Unit Editions please contact:
post@uniteditions.com

Unit 36
ISBN: 978-0-9956664-6-7

uniteditions.com

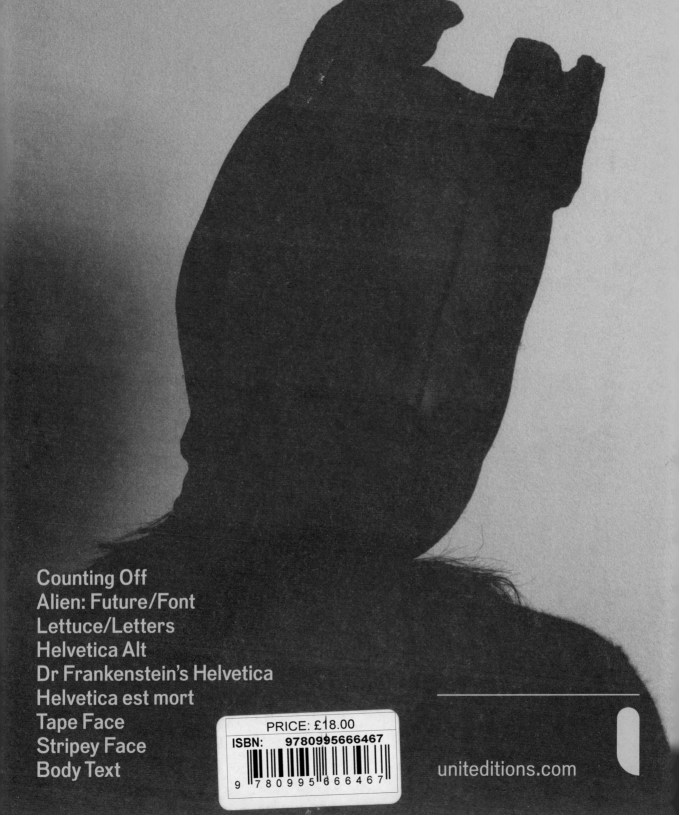

PRICE: £18.00
ISBN: 9780995666467

9 780995 666467

uniteditions.com